THE
WHITETAIL

BY
MARK E. AHLSTROM

*The author wishes to thank
Peter B. Mohn for his help in
preparing this book.*

EDITED BY
DR. HOWARD SCHROEDER
**Professor in Reading and Language Arts
Dept. of Elementary Education
Mankato State University**

**PRODUCED AND DESIGNED BY
BAKER STREET PRODUCTIONS
Mankato, MN**

CRESTWOOD HOUSE
Mankato, Minnesota

CIP

LIBRARY OF CONGRESS CATALOGING IN PUBLICATION DATA
Ahlstrom, Mark E.
  The whitetail

  (Wildlife, habits and habitat)
  SUMMARY: Describes the physical characteristics, habits, and natural environment of the whitetail deer.
  1. Whitetail--Juvenile literature. (1. Whitetail. 2. Deer) I. Schroeder, Howard. II. Title. III. Series.
XXXXXXX   1983   XXX   83-6944
ISBN 0-89686-224-0 (lib. bdg.)

International Standard Book Number:	Library of Congress Catalog Card Number:
Library Binding 0-89686-224-0	83-6944

ILLUSTRATION CREDITS:

Alan G. Nelson/Tom Stack & Assoc.: Cover
Lynn Rogers: 5, 7, 13, 16, 21, 23, 24-25, 27, 28, 31, 33, 35, 37, 39, 44
Fish and Wildlife Service: 9
Mark Ahlstrom: 10
Rick Kolodziej: 14
Steve Kuchera: 19, 43

CRESTWOOD HOUSE

Hwy. 66 South, Box 3427
Mankato, MN 56002-3427

TABLE OF CONTENTS

INTRODUCTION:

"What first caught my attention," my friend, Art, began, "was a tiny flash of light. I had climbed a tree to get a better view of a hawk on a fencepost.

"I was about fifty feet from the bird. Using my binoculars, I watched the hawk until I saw another flash. It came from the ground behind the bird. I shifted my attention to that area, but saw nothing. I kept looking back and forth, but couldn't find anything unusual. So I went back to watching the hawk.

"The bird seemed to be watching something too, and again I thought I saw some movement. I think I **felt** the movement — I didn't really **see** anything. I did know something on the ground behind the hawk had moved.

"Once more, I searched. This time I was more careful because I was really curious. The ground was covered with grass and weeds; nothing was more than a couple of feet tall. No sooner had I put my binoculars down than I saw another flash. I looked directly at the spot with the binoculars, but saw nothing. The hawk, at that point, made a slight squawk and flew off.

"As you know, Mark," Art continued, "I've spent thousands of hours in the woods. This kind of thing had never happened to me before, and I was almost mad! For the life of me, I couldn't figure out what was happening.

"At that point, I heard noise in the distance to my right. As I looked up to see what it was, I saw something move out of the corner of my eye. I quickly put my binoculars on the spot. I still couldn't make out what it was, but I could see that it was brown. And it was moving toward me **very** slowly.

"The distant noises became voices, and I saw two men heading in my direction. I returned to watching whatever it was in front of me. As I did, I again saw a flash. This time I also saw something shiny and black. That's when I figured it out.

"The shiny black thing was a nose, and the flashes had been sunlight reflecting off antlers. I had been watching a buck deer that was **crawling** on its knees

If a whitetail deer is hiding, its shiny, black nose is all you might see.

toward me in slow motion! I could hardly believe my eyes!

"The buck stopped crawling near the fencepost. He stretched out flat on the ground and froze. Even his chin was on the ground. He blended in so well with the dead grass and weeds that even I had trouble seeing him. The two men passed that buck less than ten feet away, and never knew he was there.

"That was one of my best lessons in animal survival. It's no wonder that some whitetail deer get to be huge."

Ever since my friend told me about his experience I, too, have been amazed by the whitetail deer. I've talked to experts about them and I have read everything I could about them. If I've learned anything, it is to expect many surprises from this animal.

M.E.A.

CHAPTER ONE

The deer family

The amazing whitetail belongs to the deer family. In North America, this includes caribou, elk, mule deer and whitetails. Except for size, all four are very much alike.

The whitetail is the smallest member of the deer family.

The whitetail has been given the Latin name *Odo-coileus virginianus,* partly because the first fossil of the species was found in Virginia. Scientists think there may be around thirty subspecies, or types, of whitetails, although that number seems to change a lot. It isn't easy to separate some of the subspecies.

In fact, the differences between types are so small that most people can't tell them apart. One exception is the tiny Key deer found only in Florida; another is the Coues deer of the southwestern part of the United States and northern Mexico. Both the Key and the Coues deer are half the size of the northern whitetail. But they look like any other whitetail and in many cases act the same way.

The mule deer, even though it looks like the white-tail, is very different. It requires different habitat and eats different foods. The "mulies" even behave in a much different way. Though they come from the same family, they cannot be lumped in with the whitetail.

From sea to sea

More than twelve million whitetails live in North America. That's probably as many as there have ever been. Much of the continent is home for this deer. No other large, wild animal covers as much territory.

There are more than twelve million whitetail deer in North America.

It is found all across southern Canada, in every one of the lower forty-eight states, and through Mexico to Central America.

The whitetail can live almost anywhere. It is found in deserts, swamps, the foothills of mountain ranges, forests, farmlands and prairies. Just about the only places it isn't found are in the high western mountains of Canada, the United States, and Mexico.

A neighbor

Most large, wild animals can't and won't live near man. They need a lot of land to roam. Having people around them causes stress. And, as our cities have grown, their range has declined. As the range gets smaller, so do their numbers.

The elk, caribou and mule deer all live as far from man as they can.

The whitetail deer don't seem to mind man's presence. Some of them live almost in the backyards of larger cities. Others will live in groves of trees which shelter farmsteads.

These whitetails live behind a farmer's house in southern Saskatchewan.

More than one curious whitetail has strayed into a city, has become frightened and hurt itself. In areas where they are known to live, deer crossing signs can be found along the road. One such sign can be found on a major street within the city limits of busy San Anselmo, California! Deer which "came to town" in days past didn't have a very good chance of getting back home. Usually they were shot and killed. Today, they have a much better chance. Often they can be shot with a tranquilizer dart. Once the drug docs its work, the deer can be put into a truck and taken home.

The whitetail has taken advantage of modern civilization. It knows a good thing when it sees one. To take their dinner in a farmer's cornfield is easier, and perhaps more tasty, than to browse on shoots or pick up acorns in the woods. It also has learned that it's easier to drink water from the livestock watering tank on a farm than to have to scratch for water at the bottom of a dry streambed.

In fact, the whitetail's willingness to share a part of civilization with man has caused problems. A herd of deer can wipe out a vegetable garden in one evening's feeding. And certain flowers seem like dessert to the whitetail!

As long as the whitetail has a place to hide, it can live almost anywhere. The hiding place, or cover, can be woodland, a cactus grove or merely tall weeds. The whitetail isn't picky about where it lives.

CHAPTER TWO:

How the whitetail got its name

Many a hunter has had a long day chasing the whitetail deer, only to see one or more white "flags" racing away from him as the animal or animals made their escape.

The underside of the whitetail's tail is all white. The top can be almost all brown, partly black, or almost all-black. It has the longest tail of all the deer, and it uses it as a signal. When a whitetail is alarmed, its tail is raised straight up. And usually, by the time the tail goes up, the animal is in full flight at speeds as great as thirty-five to forty miles per hour!

Other deer, seeing the "flag," don't need another message. When one tail in a herd shoots up and its owner takes off, other deer in the herd automatically do the same. It's a matter of run first and wonder why later.

Some people believe that the tail signal is also used to tell a predator that it has been seen by the deer, and might as well give up.

12

This whitetail buck has been alarmed. It's white tail, or "flag," has been raised, and the deer is running away at full speed.

Antlers

The whitetail male, called a buck, has growths on its head, called antlers. The females, called does, don't have antlers. Bucks use the antlers to defend themselves against predators, and to fight other bucks during the breeding season.

The older and healthier the buck, the larger the antlers grow. The size of their antlers is determined by the "points," or prongs, they carry.

This buck has eight-point antlers. The deer is probably at least four or five years old.

Toward the end of his first summer of life, a young buck will develop two knobs on his skull between his ears. By the end of the next summer, he probably will have single points, called "spikes." In later years his antlers will develop as many as twelve or more points.

Usually a buck will grow larger antlers each year. But deer with the largest antlers are not always the oldest. Like every other animal, the whitetail has to have a balanced and rich diet to grow. If a deer doesn't get plenty of good food, it can't grow big antlers.

After the mating season each year, the antlers are shed. The buck will begin growing a new set again in the spring.

Scent is important

Even though the eyesight of the whitetail is excellent, it uses its sense of smell just as much. It also makes its own scents using glands near the eye, in the hooves, and on the hind legs. All the different odors give each deer an identity. No two deer smell exactly the same — to another deer, that is. This is one of the ways that does use to tell their fawns apart when they are young.

This doe and her fawn have seen photographer Lynn Rogers. Because they couldn't smell him, they didn't run until he had taken several pictures.

The whitetail fawn quickly learns from its mother which odors are "good" and which are "bad." Just as the scent of a deer may tip off a predator as to where it is, the deer are always checking the air for the scent of a predator.

"If you are downwind from a whitetail and it sees you, there's a chance you may be able to get a little closer to it," said a wildlife photographer. "That's because, with the wind blowing toward you, the deer can't smell you. If the deer can't smell what it sees with its eyes, it may simply stand still for a while. If you happen to be upwind of the deer, and your scent is blowing toward the deer, you can forget it. The deer is likely to be gone even before you see it."

At birth fawns have very little odor, so does dare to leave them alone while they go off to feed. Scent glands develop as a fawn grows older.

Chow time!

Feeding time is danger time for the whitetail. So it eats carefully and moves around a lot. Instead of staying in one place, the whitetail browses a wide area. It takes a bite of this and a bite of that while moving almost constantly. As a result, the whitetail seldom overgrazes its range, or area it lives in, unless the food supply is low.

Moving while grazing helps the whitetail to fool its predators. It forces the predator into making a longer stalk, and the longer the stalk, the better the chance the predator will be detected. Even so, three of the whitetail's senses — vision, smell, and hearing — are distracted while feeding with its head close to the ground. That makes it easier for a predator, (usually a wolf, one of the large wild cats, or wild dogs) to get closer.

The deer's stomach is similiar to the stomach in cattle. It has four compartments. The food first goes into a section called the rumen, where it's stored for a short time. The rumen contains enzymes and bacteria which begin to break down the food.

A whitetail continues to feed until its rumen is full. However, it doesn't chew the food very much. Once the deer is full, it may leave the feeding area for some safe cover. Then, most often while lying down, it will chew its cud. The cud is small balls of food which are returned to the deer's mouth from the rumen. After the deer has chewed the cud well, the food passes through the rumen to the second stomach compartment, the reticulum, where the food is broken down further. Digestion is finished in the third and fourth chambers, the omasum and the abomasum.

They "talk" — but how?

The flag, or upraised tail, is the whitetail's most important means of telling others that something is wrong. It does, however, have other means of communication, too.

A wildlife photographer told of an experience he had. He came from downwind toward a small herd of deer. At first the herd, which was feeding, took no notice of him. When he was close enough to get a photo of the herd, he stood up straight and took a shot with his camera.

The noise of the camera shutter alerted the doe closest to him and she straightened up and stared. He held very still and his clothing blended in well with the background. She must not have seen him. Her twin fawns had stopped grazing, but when she went back to feeding they did too. The photographer took two careful steps forward, trying not to make any noise. He took another picture. Again, the noise of the shutter alerted the doe, and her head came up. This time she began to stamp one foot.

Other deer in the herd of seven or eight, then lifted their heads. Soon most of the whitetails were stamping their feet. The doe lowered her head, looking at the photographer, as if she was going to charge. He took another picture and the doe snorted.

This deer warns other deer nearby by stamping its left foot on the ground.

When the other deer heard the snort, all the flags came up. Two seconds later, there wasn't a whitetail in sight.

People who know the whitetail say that foot-stamping, usually with a forefoot, is one way it has of telling other deer something might not be quite right. The snort also has a role in warning other deer.

Most whitetail experts agree that they have only begun to understand how deer communicate. Both bucks and does make vocal sounds. Bucks have a raspy call used largely during mating seasons. Does call softly in high-pitched tones to their fawns. The fawns can make noises like young cattle.

It also is possible that deer communicate in tones too high-pitched for humans to hear.

Size = Location

A person from Minnesota, seeing a deer from Florida or Alabama for the first time, would prob-ably snort harder than any grown whitetail buck. That's because the deer from Minnesota are usually much larger than deer from the southern part of the United States. They also look different in other ways.

This happens because the whitetail grows accord-ing to three laws of nature. The first law says that the farther north, and the colder the climate in which an

On the average, these northern whitetails will be larger, lighter in color, and have shorter legs than whitetails that live in hot, humid areas of southern North America.

animal lives, the larger it is likely to be.

The second law says that the warmer the climate in which the animal lives, the longer its legs, ears and tail are likely to be. And the third says that the warmer and more humid the climate in which the animal lives, the more likely it is to be darker in color than its cousin living in a cold, dry climate.

There is a reason that these things happen. A larger whitetail, or other animal, has less body surface area than a smaller deer in proportion to its weight. Thus, a large deer can conserve more body heat when things get cold. In other words, deer in the North need to grow larger in order to survive the winter.

An animal loses most of its body heat from the extremities — its legs, ears, and tail. So the cold-weather whitetail's legs, ears and tail are shorter than its warm-weather cousins.

And hot, humid areas of the South, with tall trees shading woodlots and swamps, give better cover to a darker-colored deer. That's why the deer in hot, humid areas have darker hair than other whitetails.

Small, big, bigger

The Key deer of Florida, the smallest of the sub-species, may only grow to twenty-eight inches (71 cm) in height at the shoulders. A fully-grown adult buck may weigh no more than eighty pounds (36 kg). Many of the Key deer are even smaller. The Coues deer of the southwest is only a little larger. A Coues buck might be thirty-one inches (79 cm) tall and weigh a hundred pounds (45 kg).

But in the northern states — north of the Ohio

River and across the upper midwest into Oregon and Washington, and across southern Canada — the whitetails are much larger. In these areas a buck is usually at least forty inches (102 cm) tall, and weighs 160 pounds (73 kg). Many fully-grown adult buck whitetails in these northern areas can weigh more than three hundred (136 kg) pounds. The largest whitetail on record weighed 511 pounds (231 kg). It was shot by Carl Lenander, Jr., near Tofte, Minnesota, in 1926. Only a very few whitetails have come close to this record.

This large northern buck weighs well over two hundred pounds (90 kg). It might only be three-and-a-half years old.

It cannot be said too often that the size of deer within an area depends on the food that is available. If the whitetail is well nourished, it grows big, it grows fat, and it gets heavy. If it doesn't have the food supply, it can't grow large. This is as true for the Key deer as for the northern whitetail. If there are

At an age of six months, most northern whitetail fawns will weigh about eighty pounds (36 kg). Coues whitetail fawns of the same age will weigh only about fifty pounds (23 kg).

too many deer in an area, or if there is a shortage of food, the deer will be stunted. They will never be as large as a deer from the same general area that has good living conditions.

In all areas of North America does will be smaller than bucks of the same age.

CHAPTER THREE:

Spring — food, fawns & antlers

Spring is without a doubt the best time of the year for most deer.

When forest and grassy areas begin to "green up" after the snow melt and spring rains, deer begin to eat a lot to make up for the nutrition they lost during the winter.

Whitetail does are expecting new fawns — a single fawn if they mated for the first time and twins if they have had at least one fawn the year before. The does will chase away their fawns from last year before they have their new babies. A doe wants to be alone when she gives birth.

When the time for birth comes, the doe usually finds a quiet, sheltered place. After the fawn is born the doe licks it clean. In a matter of minutes the fawn can stand up. The tiny, spotted baby usually wastes no time in finding its mother's milk and having its first meal. Does often leave their fawns alone while they go get their own food. While their mother is away the fawns usually lie quietly in a shaded area. Their spotted coats blend well with the vegetation

Shortly after it's born, the fawn is licked clean and is able to stand up.

around them. It doesn't take long, however, before a fawn can keep up with its mother. In a few weeks it will feed alongside the doe, only occasionally nursing from its mother.

For the bucks, this is a quiet time. Bucks don't help care for the fawns. They either go off by themselves or form small groups and seek food together. As the days grow longer, their new antlers begin to grow. The antlers are covered with a soft layer of

This buck's antlers are covered with velvet.

"velvet." The growing antlers seem tender, and bucks avoid banging them against solid objects. If the growing antler is damaged, it may become deformed. The antlers can branch out in strange ways. In extreme cases antlers have grown around a buck's mouth. Such deformities have made bucks unable to eat or chew their food. In time, the deer may starve to death.

The whitetail fawn is, perhaps, in its greatest danger period during the spring. More than one person, seeing a fawn laying or sleeping in the grass, has thought that its mother had abandoned it. Some fawns have been taken away by people. This is a mistake. Wildlife experts urge people to leave every wild animal baby, whether deer, raccoon or bear, alone.

Predators are the main threat to the young whitetail, because the fawns cannot yet run well. While the fawn is very young, camouflage is its greatest asset. By the time it is a couple months old, it will be able to outrun most of its predators, like wolves, coyotes, and wildcats.

Dogs are also a danger to both adult and young deer in the spring. The dogs may be strays, or just neighborhood pets which haven't been kept under control.

Summer – long, hot, & nutritious

During the summer, the whitetail prepares itself for two seasons — the mating season and winter.

Summer is an easy season for deer. Most of the time they have unlimited food supplies. And in most areas there's no problem with water.

The whitetail begins to fatten up during the summer. Food is nutritious and usually plentiful. A good layer of fat gives the deer extra insulation against winter's cold.

The bucks, especially, need to feed well to gain strength for the breeding season. Their antlers also grow larger. For the does, summer is a time for raising their young. As the fawns grow, they rely more and more on the same foods adult deer eat, and less on their mother's milk. The fawn gains more weight during its first summer than at any other time in its life.

As the fawns become more independent, you might see a whole group of them frisking around and kicking up their heels. They are learning how to cope with the world around them, and they're having fun, too. Much of the learning comes from their mother as the fawn follows her example. The most important lesson is learning how to hide from predators.

Late in the summer all deer begin to grow a second layer of fur. Each hair in the new layer is hollow. The

Fawns quickly learn to feed themselves and to escape danger.

hollow hair will keep them warm during the coming winter. The fawns begin to lose their spots as their winter coats begin to grow.

Early in the autumn, as the days begin to grow shorter in length, the adult bucks start to get restless. The mating season is about to begin, and they can sense it. The older bucks begin to live alone. They will soon fight with each other over the does.

Fall — rutting and hunting

If the whitetail feeds well during summer, the fall is even better. Natural foods ripen along with farm crops. The deer will feed on both. Oak trees drop their acorns, and many deer may leave alfalfa and cornfields to munch on the acorns.

Whitetails may invade orchards to feast on ripening apples.

They will eat every apple they can reach if they get into an orchard. Even a good, sturdy fence doesn't keep them out. They will even jump over a six foot high fence. Deer have been seen standing on their hind legs to reach fruit high up in a tree.

Deer can do great damage in an orchard. It isn't just because they eat the apples. They may browse on the tender branches of the apple tree as well. That may reduce the tree's ability to produce fruit the next year.

By autumn most of the deer are in good condition. If, however, there has been a drought, forest fire or other natural disaster, the whitetails may not be prepared for the mating season and winter. If there has been a shortage of food, many deer will not make it through the winter.

The greatest change in autumn occurs in the bucks. Autumn is the rutting season, the season for mating.

The first signs of the rut often can be found on small trees. Early in the fall the buck's antlers harden. At that point each buck sheds the velvet on his antlers. To get the velvet off, bucks rub their antlers against small trees, scraping off some bark in the process. It's not a pretty process. Velvet is live skin. When the buck scrapes his antlers against a tree, the velvet bleeds as it is peeled off. Dried blood is what gives antlers their brown color.

During the rut, bucks often "fight" with bushes and small trees.

Once the velvet is shed, the buck gets into shape for breeding. He prepares to fight with other bucks over the does in the herd. The buck will attack bushes and trees in much the same way he might attack another buck later on. He also will stand under the low-hanging limb of a tree, hook it with his antlers, and shake it violently.

A whitetail buck in the rutting season can be dangerous to people. They have been known to attack people that come into their area during the rutting season.

Whitetail bucks in the same herd seldom fight each other. If they fight, only rarely does one get hurt. Fights are more likely when a buck from one herd tries to come into another herd to mate. Nor are young bucks likely to attack a large buck in his herd. They already know who's boss. Usually the strongest buck in a herd will do most of the breeding.

The mating season usually lasts for about sixty days. Most deer in North America mate during November and December. A mature buck will mate with as few as four or five does, or as many as twenty, during this time. Because of all this activity, it is common for a buck to lose one-fourth of his weight. This is why it is important for a buck to be in good condition when he goes into the breeding season.

Bucks use small trees to scrape the velvet from their antlers. The "rub" marks can be seen on the trees on the left.

Enter the hunter

Most deer hunting seasons begin during, or shortly after, the rutting season. The whitetail uses speed as a defense against the hunter, but it may also use its ability to be clever.

Many hunters walk right by the deer they are trying to hunt. A Minnesota game warden told of watching some hunters. On opening day he was standing on a hill looking down on three young bucks in a field. A team of nine hunters came into the field.

One of the bucks laid flat on his belly in some weeds. The other two bucks were standing in some tall brush and they froze. They didn't move a muscle, or even an eyelash. One of the men went right between the two standing deer and didn't see a thing. If a couple of the other men had been a foot or two to the right or left, they'd have tripped over the buck that was lying down. Once the hunters were a good fifty yards beyond them, the bucks ran off in the other direction.

Many hunters in northern states hope for snow during the deer season because it makes the whitetail easier to track. But even though a hunter may have ideal conditions, it's no guarantee he will get his deer. The whitetail is a clever animal.

Winter — season of survival

Cover, or protection from the winter winds, and food are the whitetail's first concerns in the winter.

The normally free-ranging whitetail may "yard up" in the winter. This means that they stay in one sheltered area, called a deer yard, much of the time. The deer may have to move from the area to feed, but they will return to the yard afterward. Several whitetails will share the same yard.

Heavy snow may cause the whitetail to stop moving around for a time. It's at a disadvantage, because

Deep snow makes it difficult for the whitetail, especially small ones, to escape from predators.

its hooves are not made for running across the tops of snowdrifts. The deer must plow through deep snow. This gives predators an advantage, because they can often run on top of the snow and easily chase down a deer. So whitetails try to hide when the snow gets deep.

Winter is the time during which many of the weaker, sicker, and older members of the whitetail herd are killed by their predators. Whitetails of the southwest and west are sought by coyotes and cougars. In the north, wolves and coyotes prey on deer. Packs of wild dogs may kill deer in all areas.

Surviving the winter means the whitetail must search harder for the food it needs. The food it is able to find may not be as nutritious as it was during the fall.

However, the whitetail seems to find good food if it is available. An Iowa farmer talked about the year there was an early snowfall. He was unable to pick one fifty to sixty acre field of corn. The farmer thought that every deer in Iowa must have found out about it. One of his kids rode out to the field on her pony one day in January. She stopped counting the deer when she got to fifty, and felt that there must have been at least twenty more.

Whitetails less lucky than these Iowa deer browse a lot, eating the ends of low-growing tree branches and shrubs.

A hungry whitetail will eat almost anything to fill

its stomach, even if the food has no real value. This habit is not always best for woods and forests. Foresters have said that whitetails have damaged, and even killed, parts of forests. Usually this happens only when there are too many deer in the area. It is also a sign that the deer herd is in danger of starving to death. A herd with the right number of deer in it wouldn't do this kind of damage. It would be able to find other kinds of food to survive.

When deer "yard up" they do so because they have to do it, not because they want to do it. They yard up to get out of cold winter wind. Large groups of deer will move into low areas that are out of the wind. Being so close together in these deer yards makes them uneasy. Whitetails, unlike mule deer, are not herd animals. They like to be by themselves.

The stress of being crowded into a deer yard causes whitetails to fight.

The stress of so many deer in a deer yard causes them to turn on each other as they fight for the available food. Bucks turn on does, does will even turn on their own fawns, and bigger fawns will turn on smaller fawns.

Almost all deer lose some weight during the winter, but a starving whitetail will begin to use up protein from its muscles. Once that happens, the deer is in danger of death by starvation or predators.

The threat of starvation is quite common. And once it begins, the only hope is an early spring. A few of the strongest deer usually survive. If she is starving, a pregnant doe will reabsorb the fawn she is carrying. Then she can draw on the protein it offers. This is nature's way of protecting the life of a doe. If she survives, she can breed again.

Fawns suffer the most when deer starve. Of every one hundred deer that might die of starvation, it's estimated sixty to eighty of them will be fawns. This happens because fawns are last in line to get whatever food is available.

Efforts by many to provide emergency food haven't been all that successful. And in fact, these efforts are not usually a good idea. Feeding starving deer, in an area where there are already too many, often makes the problem worse. If the deer get through the winter, more fawns will be born in the spring. So there will be even more deer the next winter faced with starvation.

CHAPTER FOUR:

Whitetails and people

The whitetail can be fond of places like roads, railroad right-of-ways, and airports. The ditches and open areas provide a lot of food for deer. However, about 100,000 deer per year are killed by cars. More are killed by trains, and perhaps a few get killed by airplanes. No one knows how many more are badly injured.

As our cities have spread out, the natural habitat of the whitetail has been changed. Unlike the mule deer, the whitetail has adapted to the change instead of moving on. It makes no difference to this animal whether it browses on a suburban apple tree or a bush in the woods.

Two kinds of predators

When it comes to taking care of itself, the whitetail often does too well. Given good food, a good range and no predators, it will reproduce so well that it outgrows the amount of available food.

There are two kinds of predators: the human hunter and the wild predator. Studies done all over the country have shown that if man tries to control wild predators we will all suffer eventually.

In areas where coyotes have been shot and poisoned into near-extinction, jackrabbits and other creatures have increased in such numbers that they are now a problem.

The same happens with the whitetail. It needs the cougar, wolf, coyote, bobcat, lynx and other predators as badly as the predators need it. If predators don't control the size of deer herds, starvation is usually the result. In areas of North America that have stable coyote and wolf populations there is a natural control on the number of whitetails. In other parts of North America, hunting by man is needed to control the whitetail.

A preservationist might argue that hunting is cruelty to animals. A hunter can argue that nothing is more cruel than slow starvation.

Strangely, some of the things many people don't like to do will help the whitetail the most. These include controlled burning of woodlands, logging, hunting and the encouragement of predators.

Large, mature forests may seem to be ideal habitat for the whitetail. But they are not. The forest canopy serves as a year-around umbrella. Plants and shrubs,

Especially in winter, whitetails need open areas to browse.

on which the whitetail feeds, can't get sunlight, so they don't grow. As they stand these forests may look pretty, but pretty means nothing to a starving deer. That is why logging helps deer. After the big trees are cut down, plants and shrubs can grow. This provides better habitat for all animals.

The same is true of forest fires. A forest fire can improve habitat, rather than destroy it. Once sunlight returns to the forest floor, so do the plants which make good habitat for whitetails and other animals.

Unfortunately, given a good habitat, the whitetail is likely to create many more of its kind. In turn, all the new deer can overbrowse the land and quickly create a brand new crisis. Before long, there will be a shortage of food again. That's why the predator is needed.

In a healthy deer herd, it's common for a doe to have twins.

The outlook is good

Today, many whitetails live because we understand them better. As conservationists learn more about game management, more effort is put into things like habitat improvement. People have to realize that game managers are not fighting for the whitetail alone. If they can make things better for deer, life will also be better for almost any animal that lives in the area.

Most state game and fish departments now do far more than issue hunting licenses and permits. They are making efforts to take their game management programs to the people.

For example, firearms safety training programs are an excellent chance to get the message to young people. There is a whole new generation of hunters coming. The hunters will be able to hunt safely and be well-informed on conservation practices.

More and more hunters' groups are also taking on projects to benefit the whitetail. In doing so, these groups are learning more about what the whitetail needs to survive in healthy numbers.

Understanding what the whitetail needs for survival has taken many years, a lot of thought, and hard work. Things still aren't perfect for the whitetail, but they're getting a lot better.

**Most whitetail deer
in North America
are found within
the shaded areas.**

INDEX/GLOSSARY:

ABOMASUM 18 — *The fourth compartment of the stomach of a cud-chewing animal.*

ANTLERS 5, 13-15, 27, 33, 35 — *A branched horn that grows on the head of a male deer.*

BROWSE 11, 17, 38, 41, 43 — *To feed or graze on plants; also the plants that an animal feeds on.*

BUCK 5, 6, 13, 15, 20, 23, 27, 30, 34, 36, 40 — *A male deer, hare, or rabbit.*

CARIBOU 7 — *A North American reindeer.*

COUES 8, 22

DIET 26, 30

DOE 13, 19, 20, 26, 30, 31, 40 — *A female deer, hare, or rabbit.*

ELK 7 — *A large, moose-like deer of Northern Europe and Asia.*

ENZYMES 18 — *Chemicals in the stomach that help digest food.*

FAWN 15, 17, 19, 20, 26-31, 40 — *A deer in its first year.*

FOSSILS 8

HABITAT 8, 42, 43 — *The place where an animal lives.*

HUNTING 36

KEY DEER 8, 22

MATING 13, 15, 34

MULE DEER 7, 8, 39 — *A deer with long ears found in western North America.*

OMASUM 18 — *The third compartment of the stomach of a cud-chewing animal.*

PHYSICAL CHARACTERISTICS 20, 22, 23

PREDATORS 12, 13, 16, 17, 29, 37, 38, 40-42, 44 — *Animals that hunt and eat other animals (called prey).*

PRESERVATIONIST 42 — *A person who believes that man should not control nature.*

RANGE 8-10, 17, 41, 46 — *The area an animal naturally lives in, that provides food and shelter.*

RETICULUM 18 — *The second compartment of the stomach of a cud-chewing animal.*

RUMEN 18 — *The first compartment of the stomach of a cud-chewing animal.*

RUT 32-34 — *The mating season of the deer family.*

SCENT GLANDS 15

SENSE OF SMELL 15

STALK 17 — *To sneak up on an animal.*

STARVATION 40, 42 — *Dying from lack of food.*

STOMACH 17, 18

SUBSPECIES 8 — *The different kinds of animals that make up a species, or family of animals.*

TAIL 12, 18

TRANQUILIZER 11 — *A drug used to relax an animal.*

VELVET 29, 33-35 — *A soft, fuzzy skin that covers growing antlers.*

READ AND ENJOY THE SERIES:

THE
WHITETAIL • THE
PHEASANT

THE
BALD EAGLE • THE
WOLVES

THE
SQUIRRELS • THE
BEAVER

THE
GRIZZLY • THE
MALLARD

THE
RACCOON • THE
WILD CATS

THE
RATTLESNAKE • THE
SHEEP

THE
ALLIGATOR • THE
CARIBOU

THE
CANADA GOOSE • THE
FOXES